Lila and Andy learn about Cars

Kenneth Adams

Book Cover by Kenneth Adams
Illustrations by Kenneth Adams
First Edition 2025

ISBN: 978-1-998552-15-3

You don't have to be the best.
You just have to do your best.

This book belongs to:

_____

Good day, friends! I'm Lila, and this is my brother Andy. We love learning how things work, and we love it even more when we get to share interesting facts with you!

Today, we're excited to tell you about cars! Whether you're riding in the back seat on a road trip with Mom and Dad or watching race cars zoom by on TV, if you're as curious as we are, you must have tons of questions about what makes them go!

So buckle up and join us as we explore everything that keeps cars moving. From wheels and engines to batteries and brakes, we're going on a fun ride today!

Cars may seem like one big machine, but they're actually made up of thousands of parts working together in different ways. To make it easier to understand how cars work, we can organize these parts into six main groups.

1. <u>Movement</u> – These are the parts that help a car move.

2. <u>Power</u> – This is where cars get their energy to run.

3. <u>Safety</u> – These are the parts that make cars safe.

4. <u>Comfort</u> – These are the parts that make sure car rides are enjoyable.

5. <u>Body</u> – The body of a car holds everything together.

6. <u>Breathing</u> – Just like people, cars need to "breathe" to stay healthy.

Each part plays a role in making cars safe, powerful, and fun to drive. Let's explore how they all come together!

MOVEMENT

The Parts That Make Cars Go

THE BASICS OF CAR MOVEMENT

Cars are incredible machines with thousands of parts that work together to help us get around. A typical car has about 30,000 parts, which work in special groups to make the car move, stay safe, and keep everyone comfortable.

The parts that make a car move include everything that helps turn power into motion. This happens through a chain of parts starting at the engine and ending at the wheels. They work as a team to control speed, direction, and stopping power, ensuring everything runs smoothly.

Each part plays an important role in this process. When you remove one of the parts, the whole system comes to a standstill.

The Wheel.

A Rim.

Treads on a tire provide traction on the road.

Did you know that a typical car wheel spins about 800 times to travel just one mile?

WHEELS

Now that we know cars move by turning power into motion, let's start with the part that actually touches the road.

The wheels connect the car to the road. A wheel consists of a metal rim that attaches to the car and a rubber tire that fits around the rim and makes contact with the road.

Tires have special zig-zag patterns called treads that help the wheels grip the road in all kinds of weather. These patterns push water away when it rains and help the car stay steady on snowy or icy roads.

During long road trips, the wheels spin hundreds of thousands of times, so it's important to make sure they are in good condition. Check the tires before every journey to make sure they have enough tread and pressure to keep the car safe.

Different seasons require different tires. Summer tires are perfect for warm weather and grip well on dry and wet roads. Winter tires are built for the cold and snow, with deeper treads and special rubber to keep you steady on icy roads. All-season tires are a combination of both, but they might not be as good as the specialized tires in extreme weather.

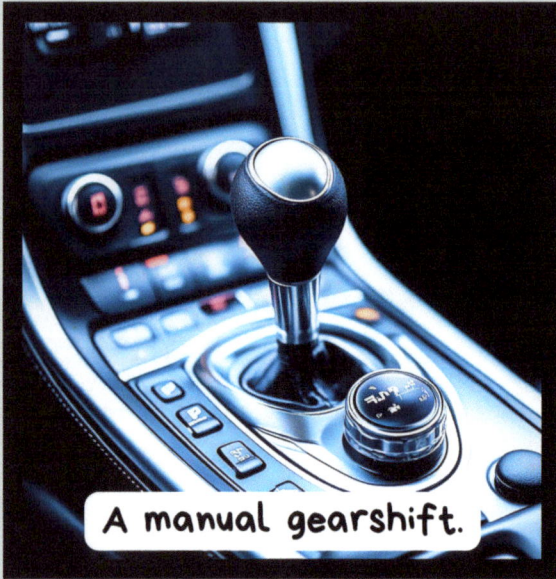
A manual gearshift.

Did you know, the world's first automatic transmission was invented in 1921?

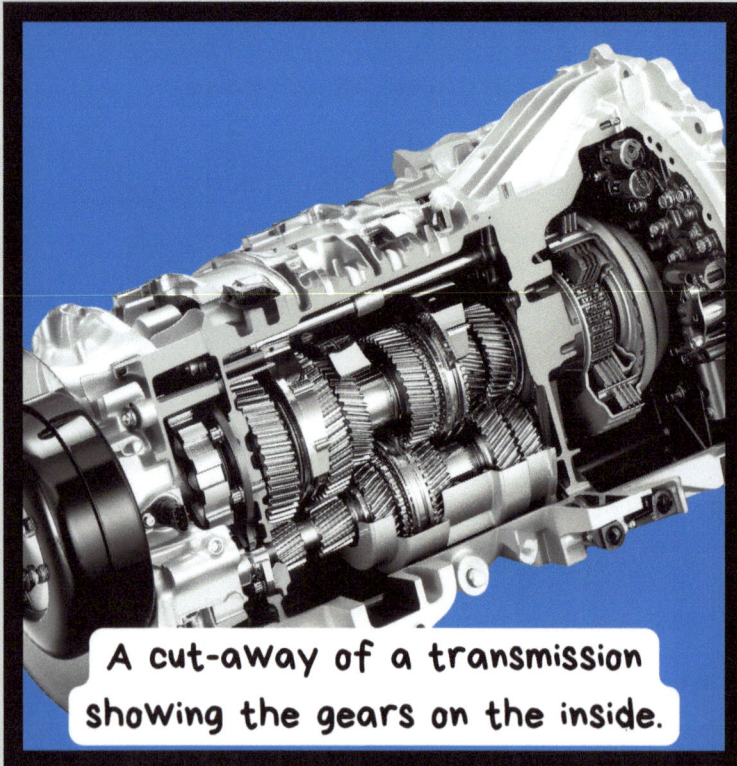
A cut-away of a transmission showing the gears on the inside.

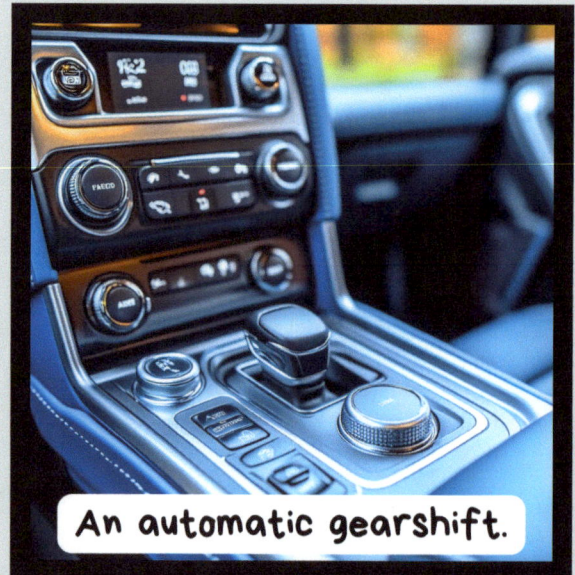
An automatic gearshift.

THE TRANSMISSION

While wheels help the car roll, they need the right amount of power to spin at the right speed. The transmission manages how the power from the engine reaches the wheels.

When starting from a stop, the transmission uses lower gears, which provide more power to get moving. As the car speeds up, it switches to higher gears, which allows it to move faster while using less energy.

Transmissions can be operated manually or automatically. With a manual transmission, the driver shifts the gears, while with an automatic transmission, the car's internal computer changes gears depending on how fast the car is going and how hard the engine is working.

Modern cars often have up to 10 different gears. Each gear has its own special job, whether the car is stuck in traffic or cruising down the highway. The transmission changes gears, adjusting the amount of power the car needs at any moment.

The transmission consists of many moving parts that generate heat when they move together. To prevent it from getting too hot, fluid is placed inside to help the parts move easily and to keep it cool. A healthy transmission shifts gears so smoothly that you can barely notice it.

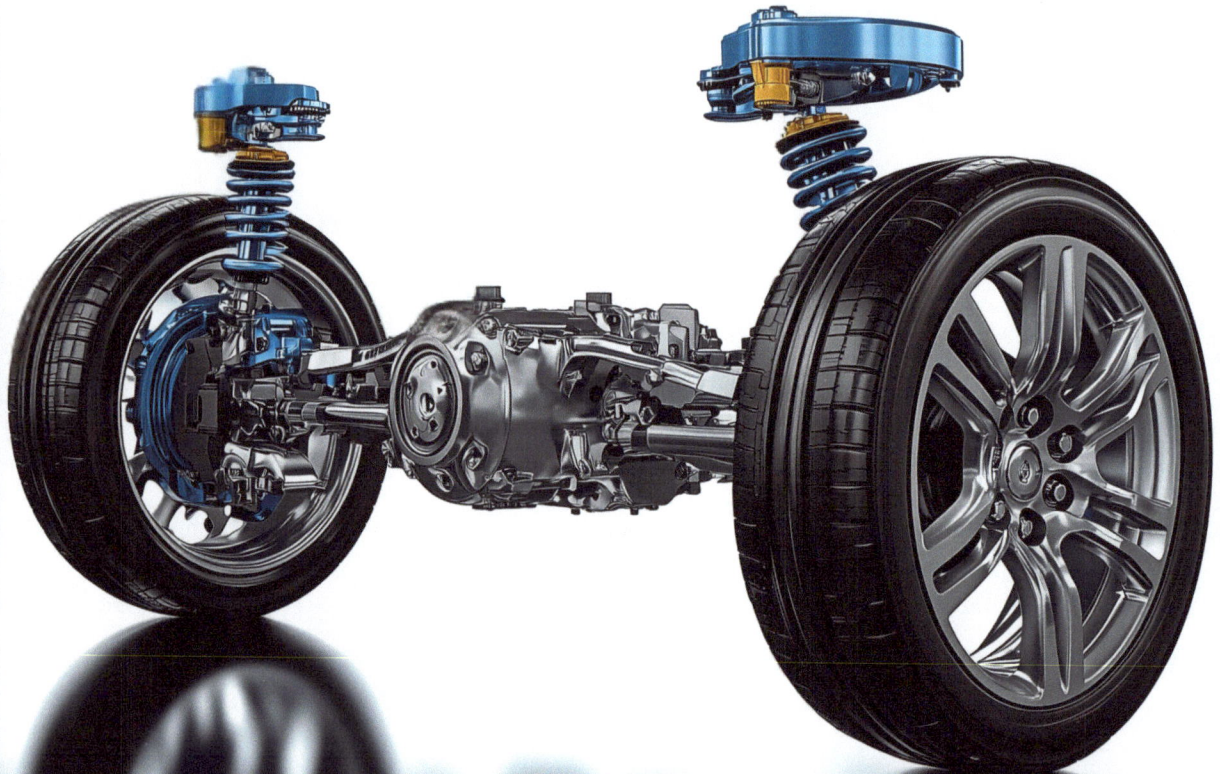

Axles connect the wheels to the rest of the car.

AXLES

The axles connect the wheels to the car, and while the transmission controls the amount of power coming from the engine, the axles carry that power to the wheels. The wheels then turn to move the car forward or backward.

Most cars have two axles, but bigger vehicles, such as trucks or vans, may have more.

At the ends of each axle, special connectors called constant velocity (CV) joints are located. These connectors allow the wheels to turn and move up and down while still receiving power from the engine. Special grease inside these joints helps them move smoothly in all directions, even when turning sharp corners.

The axles carry the entire weight of the car, so they need to be very strong. However, they also have to be somewhat flexible to deal with bumps in the road. Axles are built to be tough and durable yet light enough to handle everyday driving for many years.

Steering isn't just about turning the wheel; it's much more complicated than that. Several different parts work together to ensure that the car actually turns when you turn the steering wheel.

STEERING

Now that we have power reaching the wheels, we have to make sure the car goes in the right direction. That's where the steering system comes into play!

The steering system works with the axles and wheels to control the direction of a car. When the driver turns the steering wheel, the system works together to point the front wheels in the right direction. Controlling a car's direction is very important for keeping roads safe, so the steering system must be very precise and reliable. It is used extensively every time you drive.

Most modern cars have power steering, which makes turning the wheels much easier. This system uses either hydraulic fluid or an electric motor to help the driver turn the wheels. If a car doesn't have power steering, it will be a lot more difficult to turn the wheels, especially when the car isn't moving.

The steering system has backup systems and many safety features to keep you steering safely even if something breaks, at least until it can be fixed.

POWER

Creating and Managing Energy

THE ENGINE

The engine is the part that turns fuel into energy to make the car move. It works through something called internal combustion by doing a special four-step process over and over again.

Here's how it works:

- First, the engine takes in a mixture of air and fuel, almost like taking a deep breath. Inside a special chamber called the cylinder, a part called a piston creates a vacuum by moving down in the cylinder and sucking in this mixture of fuel and air, kind of like drinking through a straw.

- Next, the piston moves back up inside the cylinder, squeezing everything together into a tiny space.

- Then, a spark plug creates a tiny electric spark that lights the fuel and air mixture on fire. This causes a mini-explosion in the cylinder, which is so powerful that it pushes the piston back down with a lot of force.

- Finally, the piston pushes up one more time to remove all the smoke left by the explosion, pushing it out into the exhaust system.

This whole process repeats over and over, hundreds of times every minute!

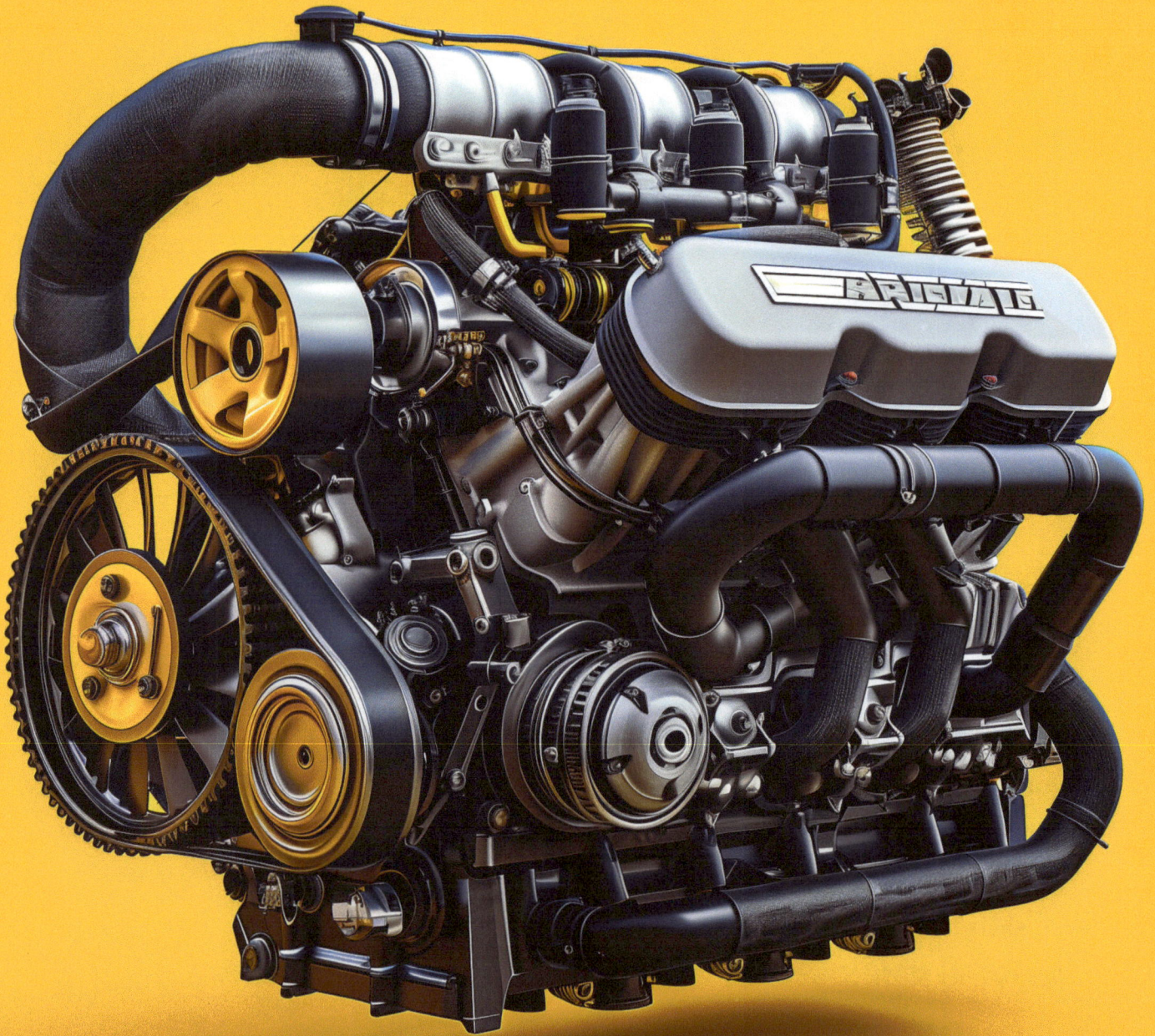

THE ENGINE

The throttle controls the engine's speed by changing how much air and fuel gets sucked in at the start. The more you press the gas pedal, the more fuel and air get mixed, and the faster your car goes.

Most car engines have four to eight cylinders working together. The pistons inside these cylinders move faster than the eye can see, working together to create the engine's power.

The engine needs to stay at just the right temperature to work correctly. If it gets too hot or too cold, it may fail. Engine coolant is a liquid circulated through the engine to maintain the perfect operating temperature, while oil keeps all the moving parts working smoothly.

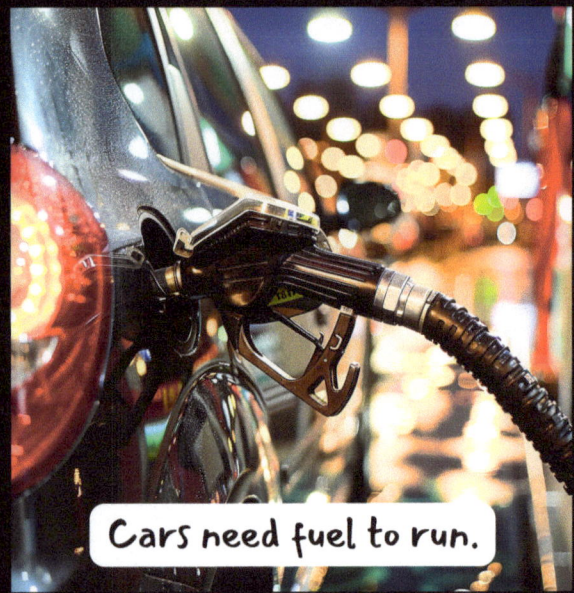
Cars need fuel to run.

Did you know some modern cars don't have a gas cap? They use a special seal to prevent fuel from evaporating!

Did you know electric cars don't need a fuel tank at all? They run on powerful batteries instead of gasoline!

A fuel tank.

THE FUEL SYSTEM

An engine can't do its job without something that can burn. The fuel system delivers the gasoline or diesel fuel needed to power the engine. The fuel starts at the fuel tank and, through a system of pumps, filters, and injectors, works its way to the engine.

Modern cars have computers that carefully control the amount of fuel used in the engine. These computer systems change the fuel mix depending on the driver's behavior, helping the engine run better and producing fewer exhaust fumes.

The fuel tank has special safety features to prevent leaks and spills. It is also designed to be durable and can resist damage in accidents. The entire fuel system is sealed to keep fumes from polluting the air around us.

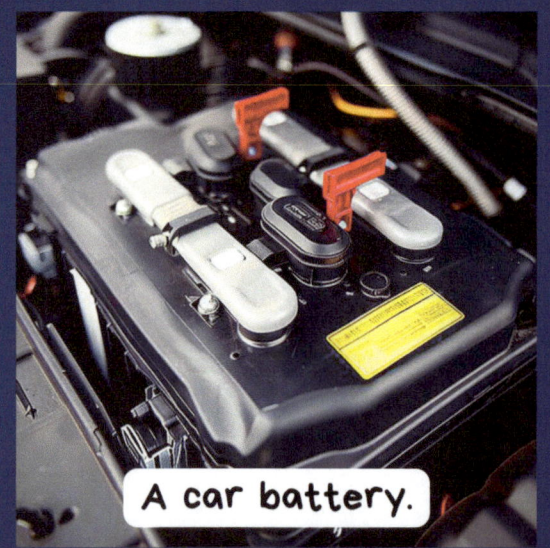

A car battery.

THE ELECTRICAL SYSTEM

Fuel isn't the only source of power in a car. While the engine needs gasoline, the car needs electricity to start, turn on the lights, and run its computers.

The car battery is a rechargeable power source that provides the electrical energy needed to start the engine and run all its electrical systems, such as the lights and radio.

While the engine is running, an alternator charges the battery. The alternator is like the car's personal power plant. It turns some of the engine's power into electricity, keeping all the car's electronics running and the battery charged. This constant charging ensures the battery has enough power to start the car and run everything electrical.

Nowadays, cars have crazy complicated electrical systems, with computers controlling everything from the engine's operation to the air conditioner (AC). These computers monitor many sensors to make cars safer and work better. The electrical system also provides power to essential safety items like airbags.

Did you know the average car battery lasts about 3 to 5 years before it needs to be replaced?

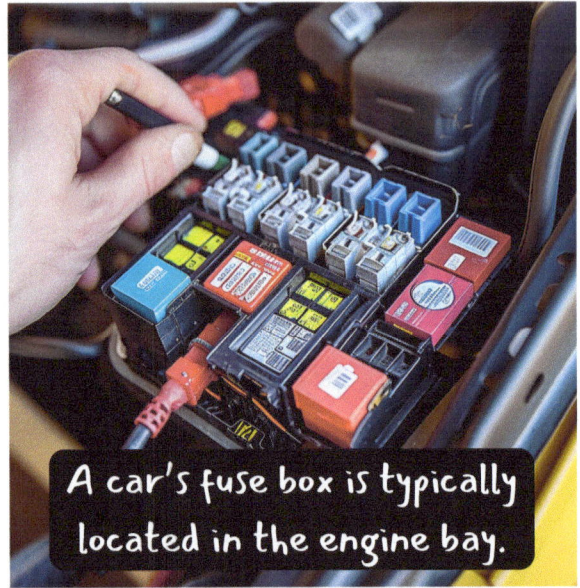

A car's fuse box is typically located in the engine bay.

Fuses come in different shapes and sizes.

Did you know, if a car fuse blows, it has to be replaced, just like a broken lightbulb? Without fuses, electrical parts like the radio and headlights could get damaged by too much power.

ELECTRICAL PROTECTION

Fuses protect the car's electrical systems from damage. These tiny devices are designed to break the electrical circuit if too much current flows, preventing damage to expensive electronic parts. Each fuse protects a specific system or group of components in the car.

The fuse box contains many fuses of different sizes and ratings. Each fuse is clearly labeled and color-coded to indicate its current rating. When a fuse breaks, it can be quickly replaced to restore power to that system while keeping other electrical components safe.

Nowadays, cars use a combination of old-school fuses and fancy electronic circuit protectors to keep things running smoothly and protect delicate electronics. Checking the fuses occasionally can help prevent electrical problems.

SAFETY

Protecting Drivers, Passengers and Pedestrians

BRAKES

A safe car needs to be able to stop quickly when needed. That's why the brake system is one of a car's most important safety features.

Modern cars use disc brakes, which work by pressing special brake pads against metal discs connected to the wheels. When the pads press against the discs, friction between them slows the car down quickly and safely.

A disc brake.

Most modern cars have anti-lock braking systems (ABS) that prevent the wheels from locking up during hard braking. Locking up is when the wheel stops turning. When the ABS detects that a wheel is about to lock up, it releases the brakes for a very short while, allowing the wheel to rotate again. The ABS then brakes again, and the process is repeated. This helps the car to stop quickly without losing control.

Airbags are designed to work with seatbelts, not replace them! Without a seatbelt, an airbag can actually be dangerous because it deploys with great force. That's why kids should always sit in the back seat, where it's safer. Buckling up every time you ride in a car is the best way to stay protected!

Also, never put your feet up on the dashboard when the car is moving. If the airbag deploys, it can push your legs back with extreme force, causing serious injuries. Keeping your feet on the floor and sitting properly is the safest way to ride!

AIRBAGS AND SEATBELTS

Brakes help stop the car, but what happens if there's an accident? That's where airbags and seatbelts come in to protect passengers.

Airbags are special safety devices that deploy faster than a person can blink to provide protection during a crash. Modern cars have airbags throughout the cabin, hidden behind panels on the steering wheel, dashboard, and sides.

Seatbelts work together with airbags to keep people safe. Modern seatbelts have special sensors that can lock the belt in place during sudden stops. The seatbelt material is designed to stretch slightly during a crash, helping to reduce injury while keeping people securely in their seats.

During a crash, sensors in the car can determine what kind of crash is happening and use that information to ensure that the proper safety features are deployed correctly to keep the people in the car from getting hurt. Together, these systems make modern cars much safer than older models. They are also constantly being made better through engineering and careful testing.

Most modern vehicles come equipped with light-emitting diode (LED) headlamps.

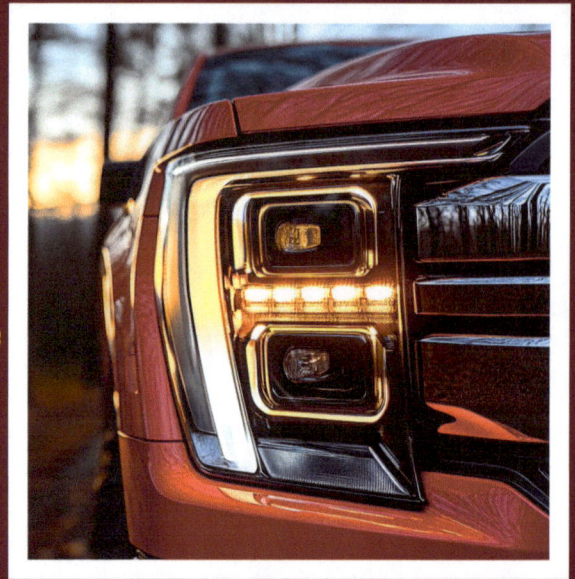

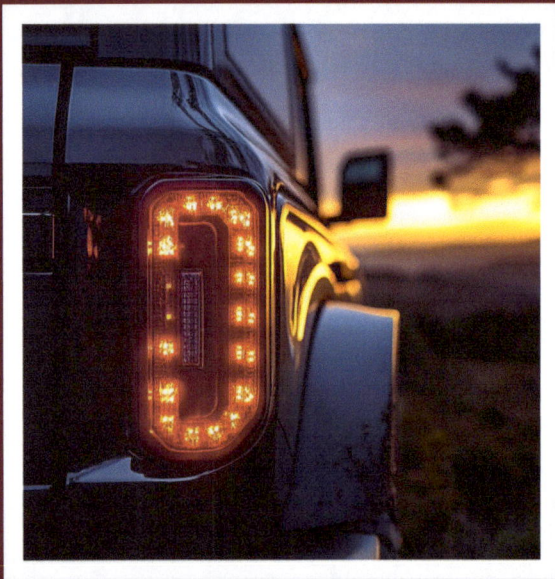

Brake lights are typically red.

The color of turn signal indicators varies between countries and can be red or amber.

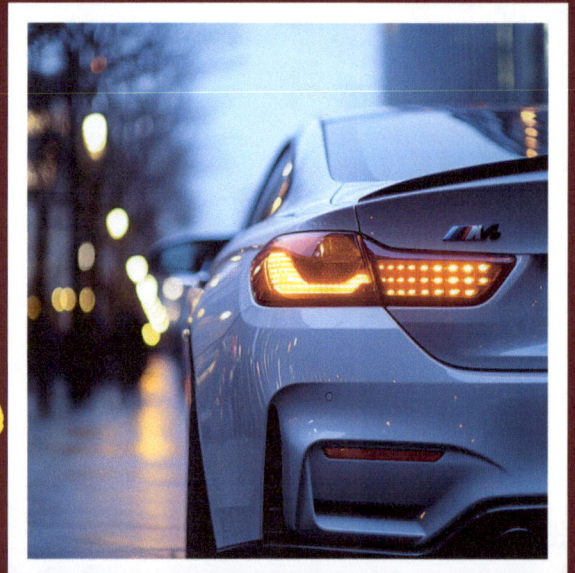

LIGHTS AND SIGNALS

Headlights light up the road at night and help other drivers see the car. Modern headlights use bright, energy-efficient LED bulbs that can last many years. Modern headlights can even move slightly when the car turns, helping the driver to see around curves in the road.

Brake lights on the back of a car warn other drivers when the car is slowing down. These bright red lights light up when the brake pedal is pressed.

Turn signals indicate to other drivers that the car is about to change lanes or turn. In some countries, they are also called indicators. These blinking amber or red lights are located at the car's front, rear, and sides so that they are visible from any direction.

Emergency flashers can activate all turn signals at once to warn other drivers of hazards on the road.

Backup cameras complement rearview mirrors to help the driver see behind the car when reversing.

The driver can adjust the side mirrors to get the best view of what's happening beside the car.

MIRRORS AND VISIBILITY

Mirrors help drivers see what's happening around them. The rearview mirror, mounted inside the windshield, provides a clear view of traffic behind the car, while side mirrors, mounted on the car's doors, help the driver see what's happening to the car's sides. All mirrors can be adjusted to accommodate different drivers and driving positions.

Modern cars have cool safety features to help you avoid accidents. Backup cameras turn on automatically when the car is in reverse, showing the driver everything behind the car. Blind spot monitoring systems use sensors to find cars the driver might not see in the mirrors, making sure you're always aware of what's around you.

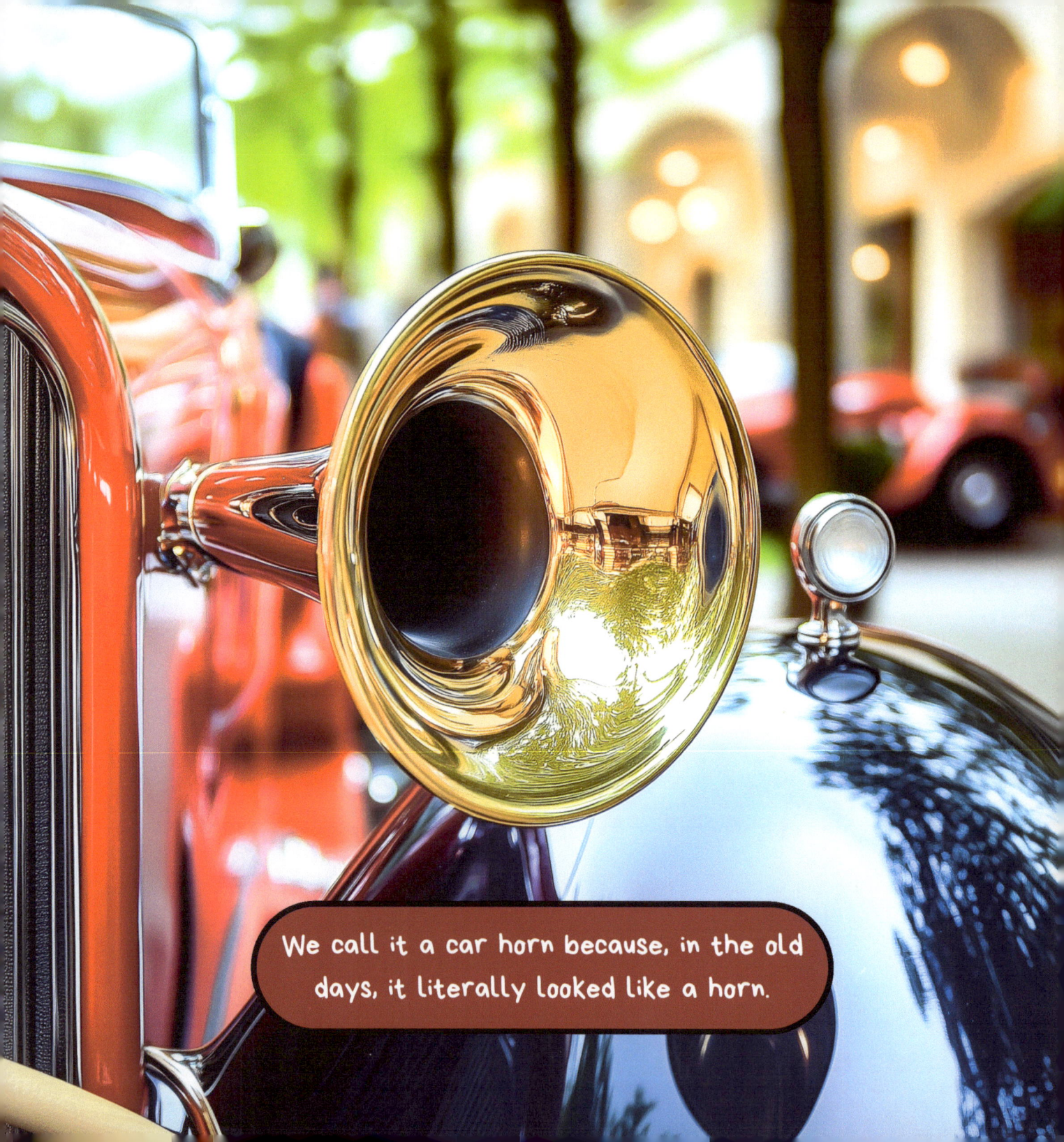

We call it a car horn because, in the old days, it literally looked like a horn.

HORNS AND SIGNALING

A car horn is an important safety device that warns others of potential danger. When the horn button is pressed, an electrical signal triggers the horn's electromagnetic system, producing a loud sound. The sound must be loud enough that people hear it and get out of the way, but it can't be so loud that it breaks any other safety rules.

Car horns are placed behind the front grille, protecting them from damage and weather. The sound travels forward to warn pedestrians and other drivers. Emergency vehicles use special horns with many different tones and sirens that can be heard from far away.

COMFORT

Making Travel Pleasant and Convenient

SEATS AND THE INTERIOR CABIN

Now that we've covered how cars keep us safe, let's explore how they keep us comfortable on long journeys!

Car seats are designed to be comfortable and safe. The frames are made from strong materials that help protect passengers during a crash, while special padding provides comfort during long drives. Modern seats can also be adjusted in multiple ways to fit different people.

Special materials in the floor, walls, and roof reduce noise and vibration from the road. This creates a quiet and peaceful environment inside the car, even when driving on rough roads.

Climate control systems maintain a comfortable temperature inside the car, no matter the season. These systems filter the air coming into the car to remove dust and pollen. Separate controls for different areas of the car allow passengers to adjust the temperature to their preference.

Seats are designed to keep you comfy and safe on long journeys.

The dashboard controls are easily accessible, so the driver won't be distracted while driving. The steering wheel buttons allow the driver to change settings, so there's no need to take their eyes off the road!

THE DASHBOARD AND CONTROLS

A comfortable ride isn't just about soft seats. It's also about having easy-to-use controls. That's why the dashboard is designed to keep everything a driver needs close by.

The dashboard is located in front of the driver. It's also called the instrument panel because it shows the driver important information, such as the vehicle's speed, engine status, fuel level, and warning indicators.

Switches and buttons that control various systems, such as the lights, wipers, climate settings, and entertainment system, are arranged to be easily accessible to the driver.

The steering wheel includes additional controls for commonly used features, allowing drivers to adjust settings while keeping their hands on the wheel at all times.

Carmakers use a combination of hydraulic cylinders and springs to reduce the impact of uneven roads on cars.

Older vehicles, as well as vehicles carrying heavy loads, still use leaf springs to make the ride as smooth as possible.

THE SUSPENSION SYSTEM

The suspension system absorbs bumps and vibrations from the road to create a smooth, comfortable ride. Shock absorbers and springs work together to control how much the car's body moves up and down while driving. This system also helps keep the tires in contact with the road for better control.

Different types of cars have different suspensions. Off-road vehicles have rigid suspensions for better handling on rough roads, while luxury cars use soft suspensions for a smoother ride. Some modern vehicles even allow you to change the suspension based on the road conditions.

A car's suspension helps make the ride smooth, but what about the structure that holds everything together? Let's take a closer look at the car's body and frame.

BODY

Structure and Protection

THE CHASSIS

The chassis is the main structural support of the car. It's like a car's skeleton, holding everything together, including the engine, suspension, wheels, and seats!

The chassis is made using different metals and construction techniques to make it very strong and lightweight.

Did you know the first cars had a chassis made of wood, just like a horse-drawn carriage?

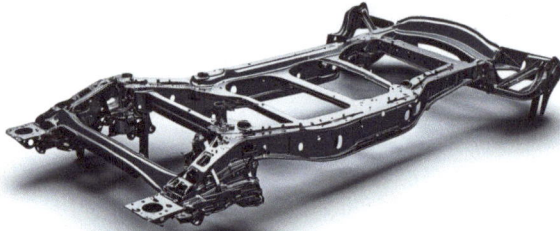
A car chassis.

Did you know trucks and SUVs often have body-on-frame chassis, making them extra strong for carrying heavy loads!

The monocoque frame of a modern vehicle.

FRAME AND STRUCTURE

The frame supports all other components and provides strength and protection to the occupants. Modern cars use special steel and aluminum alloys to create a strong but lightweight structure.

Computers help engineers design the frame to absorb energy during a crash while maintaining a protective space for passengers.

Car frames are designed to be strong and aerodynamic. Aerodynamic means the car's shape helps it move through the air efficiently, which reduces fuel use and wind noise.

Crash testing helps engineers make car frames safer. Test vehicles are equipped with sensors that measure forces during controlled crashes. This information helps designers improve how cars protect passengers in different types of accidents.

Windows allow occupants to see all around them. They can drive safely while also enjoying the world around them.

Strong door frames help to keep people safe in car crashes.

WINDOWS AND DOORS

A strong car frame protects passengers, but the parts we use to get in and out, like doors and windows, also play a big role in safety.

Car windows are made from special safety glass that breaks into small, rounded pieces instead of sharp shards. The windshield uses laminated glass, which stays together even when broken. Laminated glass consists of multiple layers of glass glued together by a layer of plastic.

Side windows use tempered glass, which is made by heating and rapidly cooling regular glass. This process makes the glass stronger, safer, and more durable.

Special locks and hinges keep doors securely closed while allowing them to open easily when needed. Strong beams inside doors protect passengers when other cars accidentally hit them from the sides.

BREATHING

Essential Operating Systems

THE EXHAUST SYSTEM

Just like people breathe in air and breathe out carbon dioxide, cars need a way to release the gases produced by the engine. That happens through the exhaust system.

Hot exhaust gases flow through special pipes starting at the engine, which help reduce noise and remove harmful substances. The exhaust system is securely attached underneath the car, where special hangers allow the pipes to expand when they are hot. The exhaust fumes are transported to the back of the car, where they are released into the atmosphere.

Modern exhaust systems include a catalytic converter that helps clean engine emissions. This device uses a chemical reaction to change harmful exhaust gases into less harmful ones before they leave the car.

Did you know that a car engine can reach temperatures of over 200ºC (392ºF)? That's hot enough to bake a pizza!

Radiators keep a car's engine from overheating by circulating coolant through tiny tubes.

A Radiator.

Make sure there is sufficient coolant in the tank.

Did you know that the world's first car air conditioner was introduced in 1939, but it was so big, it took up half the trunk?

THE COOLING SYSTEM

While engines produce power, they also generate a lot of heat. If they get too hot, they can break down. That's why cars have a cooling system to keep the temperature just right.

The engine's cooling system circulates liquid coolant. This coolant takes heat from the engine and moves it to the radiator. Air moving through the radiator's fins cools the liquid before it returns to the engine, keeping the engine from getting too hot and breaking down.

A water pump controls how fast the coolant flows through the system. It works faster as the engine runs faster. A thermostat keeps the engine at the right temperature by controlling how much coolant flows through the radiator.

Electric fans behind the radiator turn on when extra cooling is needed. They help cool the engine when the car is moving slowly or stuck in traffic. The cooling system is sealed to prevent coolant from escaping and harming the environment.

Air filters prevent dust from getting into the engine.

Did you know, if an air filter gets too dirty, the engine has to work harder? It's like trying to breathe through a clogged straw!

Did you know cars need different types of oil depending on the weather? Thicker oil for hot climates and thinner oil for cold ones!

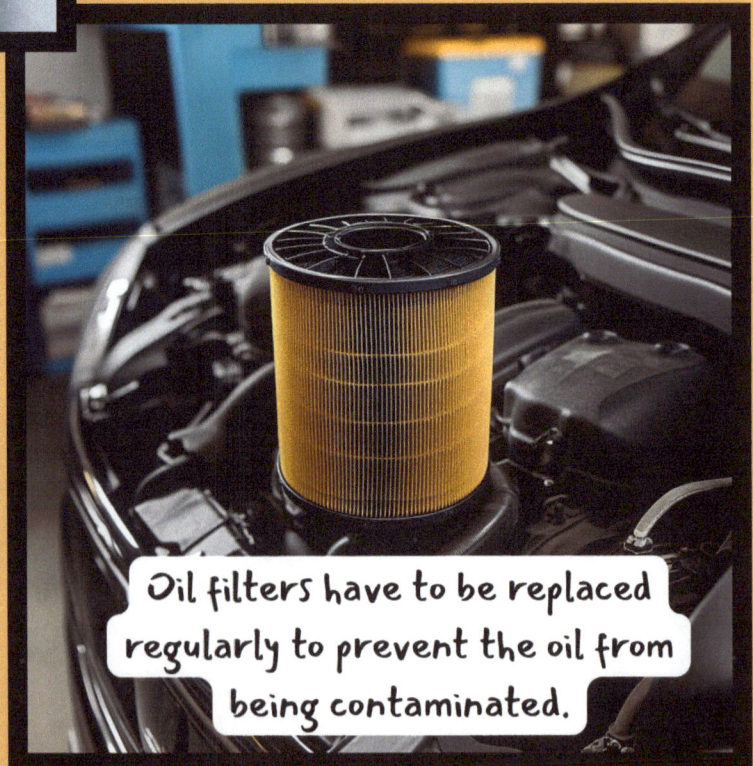

Oil filters have to be replaced regularly to prevent the oil from being contaminated.

AIR AND FILTRATION

Cars need clean air to run properly, just as people need clean air to breathe. Filters remove dust and dirt from the air before entering the engine. This clean air mixes with fuel to create the controlled explosions that power the engine.

Oil filters remove tiny particles from engine oil as it flows through the engine. Clean oil helps engine parts move more easily and protects them from wear. Oil filters are designed to trap particles smaller than human hair, keeping the oil clean.

Fuel filters keep dirt and water out of the fuel system. They are located between the fuel tank and the engine and can remove tiny particles that cannot be seen without a microscope.

In addition to protecting the engine, air filters in the passenger cabin remove dust, pollen, and other allergens from the air before it enters the vehicle.

ELECTRIC VEHICLES

HOW ARE THEY DIFFERENT?

Electric vehicles (EVs) work like gasoline-powered cars in many ways, but they have some distinct differences. Instead of an engine that burns fuel, EVs use powerful electric motors to turn the wheels. These motors get their energy from large rechargeable batteries instead of gasoline.

Since electric motors don't need gears like traditional engines, EVs often don't have a transmission with multiple speeds. Electric motors provide instant power, so EVs can accelerate smoothly without shifting gears. Many other car components, like brakes, steering, lights, and safety systems, work the same way in EVs as they do in regular cars.

EVs don't have to fill up at a gas station. Instead, they must be plugged into a charging station to recharge their batteries. Some can charge quickly at special fast chargers, while others take longer when using a regular home outlet.

Because EVs don't burn fuel, they don't produce exhaust gases, making them cleaner for the environment. Battery technology is also improving. EVs can travel further on a single charge and charge up much faster.

Cars have come a long way over the past century. All the parts of a car work together to get us where we need to go, and engineers continue to develop new technologies to make cars safer, cleaner, and more efficient.

Future cars will introduce new innovations while building on the basic principles that have made them so successful for over 100 years. Electric cars are becoming more common, using powerful electric motors and advanced batteries instead of gasoline engines. Self-driving features help make cars safer by detecting hazards human drivers might miss.

With so many exciting changes happening in car technology, what will the cars of the future look like? Maybe one day, we'll all be riding in self-driving cars or even flying ones!

Thanks for listening. We hope you enjoyed it just as much as we did. Until next time! Good Bye!

CARS

GLOSSARY

A glossary is like a mini-dictionary of terms with definitions.

Here's a glossary of terms used for Cars.

ABS (Anti-lock Braking System) - A safety system that prevents wheels from locking up during hard braking by automatically releasing and reapplying the brakes rapidly.

Air Filter - A component that removes dust and dirt from the air before it enters the engine.

Alternator - A device that converts mechanical energy from the engine into electrical energy to charge the battery and power the car's electrical systems.

Axle - A rod or shaft that connects wheels to the car and helps transfer power from the transmission to the wheels.

Battery - A rechargeable power source that provides electrical energy to start the engine and run the car's electrical systems.

Brake Lights - Red lights at the rear of the car that illuminate when the brake pedal is pressed to warn other drivers.

Brake Pads - Components in the brake system that press against brake discs to create friction and slow the car.

Catalytic Converter - A device in the exhaust system that converts harmful emissions into less harmful gases.

Chassis - The main structural framework of a car that supports all other components.

Climate Control - System that maintains comfortable temperature inside the car by managing heating, cooling, and air filtration.

Coolant - Liquid that circulates through the engine to maintain optimal operating temperature.

CV (Constant Velocity) Joints - Special connectors at the ends of axles that allow wheels to turn and move while receiving power from the engine.

Dashboard - Also called the instrument panel, displays important information like speed, fuel level, and warning indicators.

Disc Brakes - A type of brake system that uses pads pressing against metal discs to slow the car.

Electric Vehicle (EV) - A car powered by electric motors and rechargeable batteries instead of a gasoline engine.

Engine - The power unit that converts fuel into mechanical energy through internal combustion.

Exhaust System - Series of pipes and components that channel and clean engine emissions before releasing them.

Frame - The structural skeleton of the car that provides strength and protection.

Fuel Filter - Component that removes impurities from fuel before it reaches the engine.

Fuel System - Network of components that store and deliver fuel to the engine.

Fuse - Safety device that breaks an electrical circuit if too much current flows to prevent damage.

Gears - Components in the transmission that control power delivery from the engine to the wheels.

Headlights - Lights at the front of the car that illuminate the road ahead.

Horn - Safety device that produces a loud sound to warn others of potential danger.

Instrument Panel - See Dashboard.

Internal Combustion - Process where fuel and air mixture is ignited inside engine cylinders to create power.

LED (Light-Emitting Diode) - Energy-efficient bulbs used in modern car lighting systems.

Mirrors - Devices that help drivers see behind and beside the vehicle, including rearview and side mirrors.

Oil Filter - Component that removes particles and contaminants from engine oil.

Piston - Moving component inside engine cylinders that helps convert fuel explosion into mechanical motion.

Power Steering - System that makes turning the wheels easier, using either hydraulic fluid or an electric motor.

Radiator - Component of the cooling system that helps remove heat from engine coolant.

Rearview Mirror - Mirror mounted inside the windshield that provides a view of traffic behind the car.

Seatbelt - Safety restraint that keeps passengers secure in their seats.

Shock Absorbers - Part of the suspension system that helps control the car's movement and provide a smooth ride.

Side Mirrors - Mirrors mounted on car doors to help see adjacent lanes.

Spark Plug - Device that creates an electric spark to ignite the fuel-air mixture in engine cylinders.

Springs - Components in the suspension system that help absorb road bumps and maintain vehicle height.

Steering System - Collection of components that allow the driver to control the car's direction.

Suspension - System of components that absorbs road irregularities and provides a comfortable ride.

<u>Thermostat</u> - Device that regulates engine temperature by controlling coolant flow.

<u>Throttle</u> - Controls engine speed by managing how much air and fuel enters the engine.

<u>Tire</u> - Rubber component that fits around the wheel rim and makes contact with the road.

<u>Transmission</u> - System that manages power delivery from the engine to the wheels by changing gears.

<u>Turn Signals</u> - Also called indicators, these lights indicate when a car is about to turn or change lanes.

<u>Water Pump</u> - Component that circulates coolant through the engine and radiator.

<u>Wheel</u> - Consists of a metal rim and rubber tire, connects the car to the road.

<u>Windshield</u> - Front window of the car made from laminated safety glass.

CARS

QUIZ

Multiple Choice

1. How many times does a typical car wheel spin to travel one mile?
   a) 400 times
   b) 600 times
   c) 800 times
   d) 1000 times

2. How many main groups of car parts are discussed in the book?
   a) 4
   b) 5
   c) 6
   d) 7

3. What helps the transmission move smoothly and stay cool?
   a) Engine oil
   b) Transmission fluid
   c) Water
   d) Coolant

4. Approximately how many parts does a typical car have?
   a) 10,000
   b) 20,000
   c) 30,000
   d) 40,000

5. What type of glass is used in car side windows?
   a) Regular glass
   b) Laminated glass
   c) Tempered glass
   d) Reinforced glass

6. What device changes harmful exhaust gases into less harmful ones?
   a) Muffler
   b) Catalytic converter
   c) Air filter
   d) Exhaust pipe

7. How many cylinders do most car engines have?
   a) 2-4
   b) 4-8
   c) 8-12
   d) 12-16

8. What component helps charge the battery while the engine is running?
   a) Starter
   b) Alternator
   c) Generator
   d) Power inverter

9. What safety feature deploys faster than a person can blink?
   a) Seatbelts
   b) Brake lights
   c) Airbags
   d) Horn

10. What kind of glass is used in the windshield?
    a) Tempered glass
    b) Regular glass
    c) Laminated glass
    d) Strengthened glass

11. The _____ manages how the power from the engine reaches the wheels.

12. Most modern cars have up to _____ different gears.

13. The _____ controls the engine's speed by changing how much air and fuel gets sucked in.

14. The _____ is like the car's personal power plant, turning some of the engine's power into electricity.

15. _____ protect the car's electrical systems from damage by breaking the circuit if too much current flows.

16. The _____ absorbs bumps and vibrations from the road to create a smooth, comfortable ride.

17. _____ helps engineers make car frames safer by measuring forces during controlled crashes.

18. A car's _____ needs clean air to run properly, just as people need clean air to breathe.

19. The _____ keeps the engine at the right temperature by controlling how much coolant flows through the radiator.

20. Electric vehicles use powerful _____ instead of gasoline engines to turn the wheels.

1. Electric vehicles typically need a transmission with multiple speeds.

2. The alternator charges the battery while the engine is running.

3. Winter tires are better than all-season tires in extreme weather conditions.

4. Modern headlights can move slightly when the car turns to help see around curves.

5. The chassis is the outer body of the car that gives it its shape.

6. Car horns are usually placed behind the rear grille of the car.

7. The brake system is considered one of a car's most important safety features.

8. Electric fans behind the radiator only turn on when the car is moving fast.

9. Side windows and windshields use the same type of safety glass.

10. Modern cars typically have computers that control the amount of fuel used in the engine.

Answer Key

Multiple Choice	Fill in the Blank	True/False
1. c	11. transmission	21. False
2. c	12. 10	22. True
3. b	13. throttle	23. True
4. c	14. alternator	24. True
5. c	15. fuses	25. False
6. b	16. suspension system	26. False
7. b	17. crash testing	27. True
8. b	18. engine	28. False
9. c	19. thermostat	29. False
10. c	20. electric motors	30. True

Take a look at other subjects Lila and Andy are learning about...

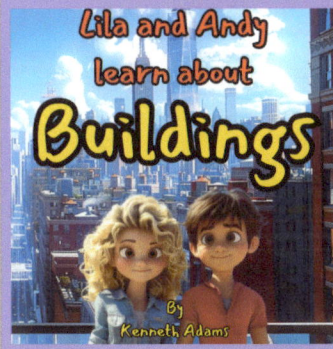

Lila and Andy learn about **Buildings** — By Kenneth Adams

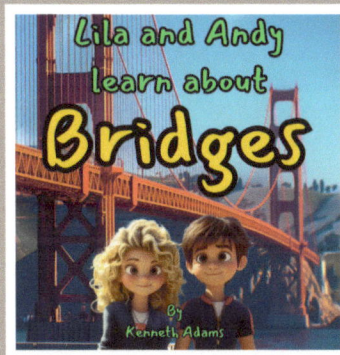

Lila and Andy learn about **Bridges** — By Kenneth Adams

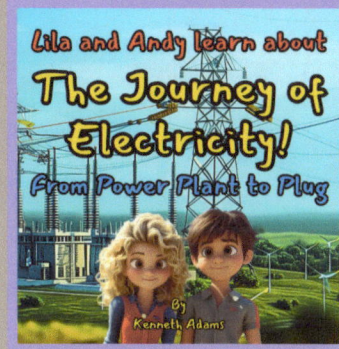

Lila and Andy learn about **The Journey of Electricity!** From Power Plant to Plug

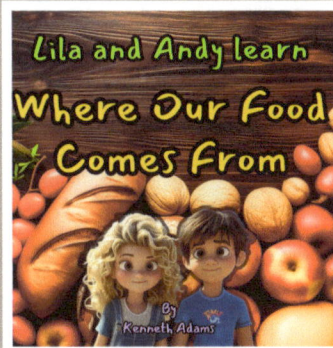

Lila and Andy learn **Where Our Food Comes From** — By Kenneth Adams

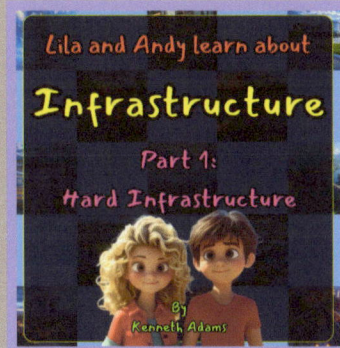

Lila and Andy learn about **Infrastructure** Part 1: Hard Infrastructure — By Kenneth Adams

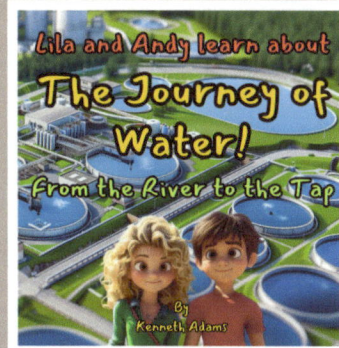

Lila and Andy learn about **The Journey of Water!** From the River to the Tap

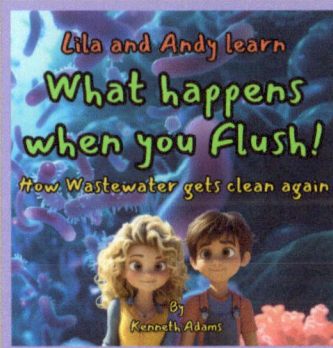

Lila and Andy learn **What happens when you Flush!** How Wastewater gets clean again — By Kenneth Adams

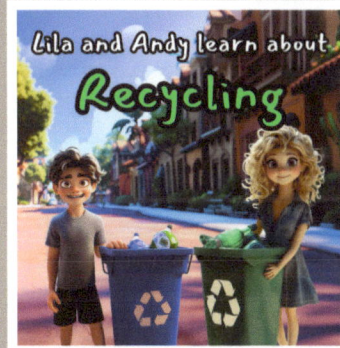

Lila and Andy learn about **Recycling**

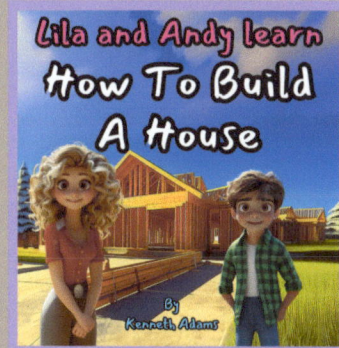

Lila and Andy learn **How To Build A House** — By Kenneth Adams

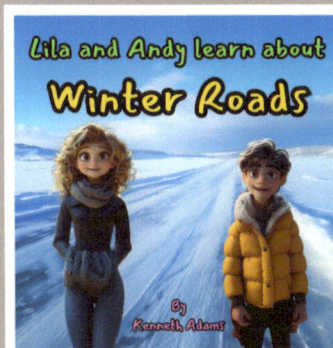

Lila and Andy learn about **Winter Roads** — By Kenneth Adams

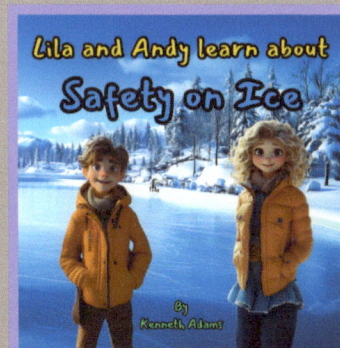

Lila and Andy learn about **Safety on Ice** — By Kenneth Adams

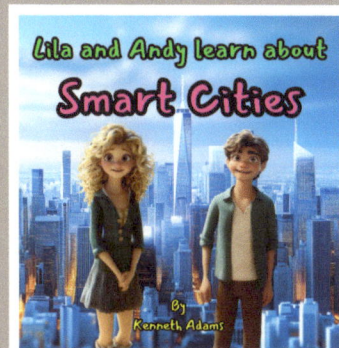

Lila and Andy learn about **Smart Cities** — By Kenneth Adams

9 781998 552153